W9-BZB-525

FRITZ HIRSCHBERGER

The Sur-Rational Holocaust Paintings

Edited by
Stephen C. Feinstein

Center for Holocaust and Genocide Studies
University of Minnesota

Conception, research and texts:
Stephen C. Feinstein and Fritz Hirschberger

Design and editing:
Constantin Parvulescu

Published through The Center for
Holocaust and Genocide Studies,
University of Minnesota, with the
cooperation of The Regis Foundation,
Minneapolis, Minnesota, USA.

Ownership of the paintings of Fritz
Hirschberger and rights to publication are
held by The Regis Foundation.

Websites on Hirschberger:
http://chgs.hispeed.com/Visual___Artistic
_Resources/Fritz_Hirschberger/fritz_hirsc
hberger.html

http://chgs.hispeed.com/Visual___Artistic
_Resources/Fritz_Hirschberger2/fritz_hirs
chberger2.html

© 2002 The Regis Foundation, Minneapolis,
Minnesota, USA
ISBN 0-971-8290-0-4
Printed by South China Publishing
Company, New York and Hong Kong

Cover: *Indifference* (oil on canvas,
40"x60")
Page 3: *Self-portrait of the Artist With His
Father* (oil on canvas, 40"x60")

Foreword

The terrorist events of September 11, 2001, not only marked a new era in history, but also challenged the artistic imagination. Mel Gussow, a reporter for The New York Times, asked the uncanny question: "How do artists respond to momentous acts of violence?"[1] What he termed "the art of aftermath" was already emerging less than two months after the tragedy. Clifford Chanin, founder and president of The Legacy Project, noted the importance of prior violent events like the Holocaust and Hiroshima for understanding the present and its creative discourse. The crucial issue is "the conflict between the fading of memory and the need to remember."[2] In what form will remembrance emerge when witnesses are gone?

The Holocaust in particular poses some tough questions about representation. At one extreme are the documents witnessing destruction, some written and some photographic. There are also the eyewitness accounts, now being stored into major archives. And then there is the response. Art made in the concentration camps and ghettos is still considered valid as a form of artistic memoir, although the quality of such art, produced in extreme conditions, varies greatly. The artwork of survivors has also been questioned. How truthful, how well preserved is their memory?

More recent artistic endeavors, however, depend on secondary knowledge, especially on photographic images. The painter Fritz Hirschberger, a victim of the Nazi regime and a survivor who fought with the Polish Anders Army, understood the challenges posed by representation. He was clear in emphasizing that his two series of paintings, Indifference and The Fifth Horseman, were not derived from his direct Holocaust experience, but from his understanding of it from extensive reading and introspection. He began his inquiries after entering what may be termed his fourth life, the American one (the first three being in Germany, Poland and the Soviet Union). The loss of his family is a trauma with which Hirschberger still has to deal. He struggles to comprehend it and, if possible, to represent it.

Hirschberger realized that the problem of Holocaust-related art was the superseding of the visual cliché. He found ways of representation that dialogued with images from Christianity, from mythological and classical models, from contemporary photographs, and finally from the written text. Hirschberger's art is not a continuous narrative. He knows the complete story cannot be told. However, as fragments, his paintings provide the viewer with another way—alternative to history and literature—to understand this dark event, and to help answer the question of how future generations may remember it. His way is the sur-rational.

University of Minnesota's Center for Holocaust and Genocide Studies is grateful to The Regis Foundation for underwriting support for the display of the Hirschberger paintings and the publication of this album.

Stephen C. Feinstein
Center for Holocaust and Genocide Studies
University of Minnesota, Twin Cities

---

[1] Mel Gussow, "The Art of Aftermath, Distilled in Memory," *The New York Times*, November 14, 2001, page E1.
[2] Clifford Chanin as quoted in *Ibid*.

The Sur-Rational Experience

Fritz Hirschberger was born in Dresden, Germany, in 1912. His father came from the Austrian partition lands of Poland in Galicia, and his mother from Bohemia. Both were Jews. During the 1930s, Hirschberger received a traditional liberal arts education in Dresden. He developed affection for the painting of the Renaissance, especially the works of Giotto and Dürer, as well as for the German expressionists of the 1920s, for what later became known as "degenerate" art. In October 1938, as Nazi Germany began to cleanse itself of undesirable aliens, Hirschberger and his family were expelled to Poland, his father's "native" land.

Fritz Hirschberger with Basia, Ancona, Italy, 1946.

In Krakow, Hirschberger learned Polish, an alien language to him as he had been raised with German as his native tongue. He became an organizer for the Zionist Revisionists led by Vladimir Zeev Jabotinsky. The Zionist Revisionist organization, "Betar," wanted the immediate establishment of the Jewish State in Palestine. Hirschberger was called up for duty in the Polish Army just before the outbreak of the war with Germany. By September 15, 1939, his division no longer existed. He fled, like many other Polish citizens and soldiers, to the Soviet Union. There he was arrested for possessing the membership card in a Zionist organization and was given a twenty-year sentence in what Alexander Solzhenitsyn would later call "The Gulag Archipelago." Hirschberger was sent to Kolyma, in the Komi Soviet Republic, within the Arctic Circle. His chances of survival at this time were slim. An accident of history saved him.

On June 22, 1941, Germany invaded the Soviet Union. Inmates like Hirschberger were declared "political prisoners" and were released on the promise of joining either the Soviet Army or the Polish "Anders" Army then forming in Central Asia. Hirschberger traveled with the Anders Army through the Middle East where most of the Jewish members left to join the Palestinian forces under Jewish control. Hirschberger, however, insisted on staying with the Anders Army as he felt an obligation to the Poles who were fighting for Poland's freedom. His unit fought in the North African campaigns against General Erwin Rommel and he later participated in the Battle of Monte Cassino in Italy.

After the war, Hirschberger found out that his parents had died during the Holocaust. His father was killed at Dora, working in an underground factory for the V-2 Rocket program. Hirschberger, however, found out that his fiancé, Gisela, was alive and well in England. Being a visitor in England when the war broke out, Gisela was interned for two years on the Isle of Man. As a "German national," she was permitted to write to her parents in Dresden until they were deported and killed.

Fritz Hirschberger after El Alamein in the Western Desert, 1943.

The Hirschbergers came to the United States in 1948. Fritz worked in some engineering jobs as well as with artists from The New School on 12th Street in Manhattan. In 1984, Fritz, Gisela and their three sons moved to San Francisco. Hirschberger continues to paint in the year 2001. Gisela has also had a career as a painter.

The title of Hirschberger's first set of paintings is *Indifference - The Sur-Rational Paintings*. He explains: it embraces subjects from the Holocaust that are beyond rational explanation. "How can one understand a German commandant who presides over mass murder and then sits down to eat a chicken dinner, as if this was normal work?" Although Hirschberger's early paintings dealt with many figurative subjects, he began to paint on Holocaust in 1980, after reading about events he had missed directly, thanks to his being in military service. He became upset with the international policies of the Nazi period, whether of the perpetrators in the form of Nazi Germany, or of the bystanders like the Western Powers, including his adopted country, the United States, or even of Jewish and Zionist organizations. His paintings, in this respect, represent much of the suppressed anger that many Holocaust survivors probably experienced. This is linked to the feeling of abandonment amidst mass murder.

Puppets on a String (oil on canvas, 40" x 36").

Hirschberger is a researcher, and his paintings raise the question of what is necessary for a painting "to be" a Holocaust painting. Certainly the work of other artists, for example Hungarian survivor Alice Lok Cahana, or child of survivors Mindy Weisel, testifies to the power of abstraction. However, since Hirschberger was not in a concentration camp, his information on this period comes largely from speaking with other survivors and reading the history of the period. The result is what may be called a series of "naïve" paintings with strong color, powerful themes, and messages that have to be deciphered in a Holocaust context. With Hirschberger, there is a strong link between history and the visual representation of the Holocaust.

In April 1990, the original paintings in *Indifference* were destroyed in what is believed to be an arson fire in his studio. Hirschberger repainted them; he considers the quality of the work improved because of the process of thin layers of oil paint that he now uses in his technique. A second series, *The Fifth Horseman*, followed. It suggests his own struggle to continue learning about this dark subject and to bequeath the knowledge and visual representation to another generation.

The Sur-Rational Paints. Representing the Holocaust

The Holocaust is a subject that apparently seems to defy artistic representation. The dehumanization, humiliation, and mass-murder of European Jewry by the Nazis were an event of unparalleled proportions. Other groups such as Roma and Sinti peoples (Gypsies), Jehovah's Witnesses, homosexuals, political prisoners and opponents to the regime became part of the world of the concentration and death camps. However, in the diabolical world of Nazi race theory, only all of the Jews and most of the Gypsies were to die.

After Such Knowledge, What Forgiveness? (oil on canvas, 54" x 40")

The mass killing that took place within the framework of the Holocaust had some unique aspects that set it apart from other genocides and that authenticate the word "Holocaust" or "Shoah," in Hebrew, meaning "an offering consumed by fire." These words have religious references and impose the necessity of some sort of theological discussion of the event. Jews had been victimized for centuries by religious anti-Semitism bred within Christianity and supported by economic, social and political liabilities. However, before Hitler, Jews who were persecuted had the option of converting to Christianity or of being expelled to another land.

The attempt by artists to grapple with the Holocaust is nothing new. It is a movement that was visible during Hitler's rise and concentration of power. Marc Chagall's *White Crucifixion*, a response to *Kristallnacht* ("The Night of Broken Glass") in Germany, 1938, remains the icon

among many paintings that describes Jewish suffering before 1939. Unlike artists who merely depicted suffering, Chagall used the theme of a crucified "Jewish" Jesus set against vignettes of Jewish persecution that unfolded in the Nazi era. Artists like Yankel Adler and Ben Shahn produced strong responses to Jewish and other persecutions during World War II. Both Jewish and non-Jewish artists who were interned and perished in concentration camps produced artistic legacies of their victimization.

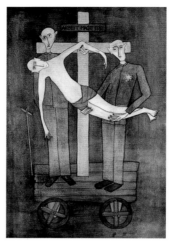

Arbeit macht frei - Work Liberates (Slogan over the main entrance to Auschwitz) (oil on canvas, 60" x 40").

There are many dilemmas related to the representation of the Holocaust. There are even statements about its being impossible to represent. One may argue the same for other traumatic experiences; this belief was the very stimulus for a tremendous outpouring of visceral art about World War I during the war and through the 1920s. Despite such taboos, especially the issue of artists simply trying to "reproduce" a memory of an event they did not experience and competition with the archival photographic record, the quest for a visual language as a means to convey memory continues. The quest, in a certain sense, is for a new language with new symbols and new metaphors. The famed writer and Auschwitz survivor Primo Levi understood this well when he said: "daily language is for the description of daily experience, but here is another world, here one would need a language 'of the other world.'" But later in his life, when commenting on Theodor Adorno's famous quote that "after Auschwitz there should be no lyric poetry," Levi said: "After Auschwitz, there should be only poetry about Auschwitz."

Survivors share a special vision of having been victims of the Holocaust. Non-survivors cannot possess the same vision. Survivors possess memories that others can comprehend only in indirect ways. In some respect, the only "authentic" Holocaust art may be said to be the art of survivors. Fritz Hirschberger's *Sur-Rational Paintings* fit into this category. The paintings represent an attempt by Hirschberger as survivor and a Jew to depict his impressions of historical events and his own emotional, and frequently cynical responses to events during the Holocaust. Using a "naive" style of representation combined with familiar themes from Christian art, plus a Renaissance-like silky finish on his oil paintings, the artist provides the viewer with unique insights into the Holocaust. The prevalence of purple hues suggests a religious-like art. Many of the paintings are provocative, but deal with real issues: how ordinary people became mass murderers while living a normal family life; how the world's political checks and balances failed because of appeasement; how Christians, including Western diplomats and the Vatican, abandoned the moral and ethical standards of the Jew, Jesus Christ, to become, for most part, inactive bystanders to the crime. While many cases of rescue are recorded, the most well known being that of Oskar Schindler because of the notoriety surrounding the film by Steven Spielberg, the numbers of rescuers were relatively small compared to the victimization. The question of indifference, which is depicted in several paintings, has a resonance into the twenty first century, as the United States debates immigration policy and how much to get involved in conflicts far from American shores, in places where genocide has a potential to explode.

Identity Card Nr. 13037 for the Jew Hirschberger Isidor* or "The Sword of Damocles" (photomontage 30" X 40").
*the artist's father, killed at Dora concentration camp

Above all, however, there is a contemporary message in Hirschberger's paintings. That message relates to a positive meaning that can come from a negative event like the Holocaust—that the problems of the contemporary world that are based on hatred, prejudice and racism can be solved only by dealing with the issues directly. Indifference cannot be accepted. Hirschberger's painting *Indifference* contains a text from the Yiddish poet Edward Yashinski, who survived the Holocaust but died in a communist prison cell:

Fear not your enemies, for they can only kill you.
Fear not your friends, for they can only betray you.
Fear only the indifferent, who permit the killers and
betrayers to walk safely on earth.

But was indifference the issue, or something else? A few historians have asserted that Germans were not indifferent, but were willing accomplices and active killers in a fanatical, but long nurtured anti-Semitism that between 1938 and 1945 tried to eliminate what was perceived to be all Jewish power in Germany, and the rest of Europe as well. Daniel Goldhagen, for example, believes the Germans pursued an eliminationist doctrine, which is quite at odds with the concept of indifference.

Hirschberger does not deal with easy themes or permit the audience to walk away from viewing his works unaffected. The second series, *The Fifth Horseman*, draws its title from the Bible, Book of Revelations 6:8: "And now I saw a pale horse, and its rider's name was Death. And there followed after him another horse whose rider's name was Hell. They were given control of one-fourth of the earth, to kill with war and famine and disease and wild animals." This is a familiar theme of the Renaissance, updated by the artist with intense color and new symbols of death that were part of the Nazi technology of mass murder.

Thus, in this series, and in the title painting of the same name, Hirschberger links the medieval image of St. George, the protector saint, the symbol of the triumph of good over evil, with that of a new horseman bearing Zyklon B gas. Underneath his horse are the names of the death camps created not in the Medieval period, but in the twentieth century, what some have now labeled as "a century of Genocide." The artist's use of the Christian saint certainly raises a deeper question of the relationship of Christian anti-Judaism in the Holocaust. Many of the Nazis were raised within the Christian tradition, but one can hardly call their actions "Christian." Yet, historic Christian demonization of Jews, recalled by Pope John Paul II in the 1998 Papal letter "We Remember," has confirmed that the Holocaust is a "Christian problem" although Jews were the principal victims.

The Last Supper at Evian or The Fish Stinks First from the Head (oil on canvas, 40" x 60").

In Hirschberger's *The Seduction of Germania*, Germania is depicted as Eve in the Garden of Eden, who has presumably given a can of Zyklon B gas to Adam, dressed in SS uniform, at the instigation of the snake, undoubtedly symbolizing Hitler. The Biblical story of original sin is also connected with the idea of individual freedom. Adam and Eve did not heed God's demands and ate the forbidden fruit, for which they were expelled from paradise. What they received in return was freedom. Freedom, in turn, suggests that humankind can make moral choices. During the Holocaust, humans were free to build gas chambers, and exterminate the victims.

When looking at the paintings reproduced in this book, one might pose the question: What is the most durable method by which the Holocaust will be remembered? Will the public and students one hundred years from now possess an intense interest in the subject, or will this history, despite its horror, become a footnote like other genocides of the past—of Native Americans, Armenians, Herreros, Bosnians, Rwandans and others. Will we be like those who sarcastically comment, "Who remembers the Albigensians?" Finally, will the historical narrative, like many other events of the past, move into the realm of visual representation, despite all of the warnings about taboos and problems of representation?

Stephen C. Feinstein

The Sun and the Moon Shine on All: *the Mute, the Blind, the Deaf* (oil on canvas, 60" x 30").

Bibliography
Books and Articles on the Artistic Representation of the Holocaust

Amishai-Maisels, Ziva. *Depiction and Interpretation.* London: Pergamon Press, 1993.

_____. "The Jewish Jesus." *Journal of Jewish Art.* Vol. 9, 1982.

Aptecker, George. *Beyond Despair.* Morristown: Kahan and Kahan Publishing Co., 1981.

Art in a Concentration Camp: Drawings from Terezin. New York: New School Art Center, 1967.

Art in Terezin, 1941-1945. Memorial Terezin, Czechoskovakia: The Small Fort, 1973.

Art Out of Atrocity: Works by Alice Lok Cahana and Robert Barsamian. Hamilton: Colgate University, 1998.

Bacon, Hannelore, Miram Beerman and Gert Schiff. *Primal Ground: Miriam Beerman, Works from 1983 to 1987.* Montclaire: Montclaire Art Museum, 1988.

Baigell, Matthew. *Jewish-American Artists and the Holocaust.* New Brunswick: Rutgers University Press, 1997.

Bak, Samuel. *Chess as a Metaphor in the Art of Samuel Bak.* Montreaux, Switzerland: Olsommer, 1991.

_____. *Landscapes of the Jewish Experience.* Essay and commentary by Lawrence L. Langer. Boston: Pucker Gallery, 1997.

_____. *The Past Continues.* Boston: David R. Godine, 1988.

Beller, Ilex. *La Vie du Shtetl.* Paris: Editions de Scribe, 1986.

Bernbaum, Israel. *My Brother's Keeper. The Holocaust Through the Eyes of an Artist.* New York: Putnam, 1985.

Blatter, Janet and Sybil Milton. *Art of the Holocaust.* New York: The Rutledge Press, 1981.

Bohm-Duchen, Monica. *After Auschwitz: Responses to the Holocaust in Contemporary Art.* Sunderland, UK: Northern Centre for Contemporary Art, 1995.

Borowsky, Irvin J. *Confronting the Inconceivable.* Philadelphia: American Interfaith Institute, 1992.

Braham, Randolph L. (Ed.) *Reflections on the Holocaust in Art and Literature.* New York: Columbia University Press, 1990.

Constanza, Mary. *The Living Witness-Art in the Concentration Camps and Ghettos.* New York: Macmillan, 1982.

Feinstein, Stephen. "Artistic Responses to the Warsaw Ghetto: Tchelitchew, Shahn and Kaliszan." *The Uses and Abuses of Knowledge.* Ed. Henry Knight and Marcie S. Littell. New York: University Press of America, 1996.

_____. "Auschwitz in the Backyard: Contemporary Polish Artists face the Holocaust." *Proceedings of the 24th Annual Scholars Conference on the Holocaust and the Churches.* Ed. Dominick Iorio, Richard Leibowitz and Marcie Sacks Littell. New York: University Press of America, 1996.

_____. "Contemporary Artists and the Holocaust." *What Have We Learned? Telling the Story and Teaching the Lessons of the Holocaust.* New York: Mellen Press, 1994.

_____. "Mediums of Memory: Artistic Responses of the Second Generation." *Breaking Crystal.* Ed. Efraim Sicher. Urbana: University of Illinois Press, 1997.

_____. "Memory and Re-Memory of the Holocaust through Installation Art." *Reclaiming Memory: American Representations of the Holocaust.* Ed. Pirijo Ahokas and Martine Chard-Hutchinson. Turku, Finland: University of Turku. School of Art Studies. Series A, No.35, 1998.

_____. "The Other Side of Memory: Toward a Typology of Holocaust Art." *Response: A Contemporary Jewish Review.* No. 68. Fall, 1997/Winter, 1998.

Feinstein, Stephen (Ed.). *Witness and Legacy: Contemporary Art About the Holocaust.* Minneapolis: Lerner Publications, 1994.

Felstiner, Mary Lowenthal. *To Paint Her Life: Charlotte Salomon in the Nazi Era.* New York: HarperCollins, 1994.

Fluek, Toby Knobel. *Memories of My Life in a Polish Village, 1930-1949.* New York: Knopf, 1990.

Freudenheim, Tom L. "Viewing Holocaust Art as Art." *Shema, A Journal of Jewish Responsibility.* No. 15/284, December 28, 1984.

Furth, Valerie Jakober. *Cabbages and Geraniums: Memories of the Holocaust.* Boulder: Social Science. Monographs (Distributed by Columbia University Press), 1989.

Gilbert, Barbara (Curator). *From Ashes to the Rainbow, A Tribute to Raoul Wallenberg, Works by Alice Lok Cahana.* Los Angeles: Hebrew Union College Skirball Museum, 1986.

Goodman, Hannah Grad. "Survivors Reject Art History." *Shema, a Journal of Jewish Responsibility.* No. 15/284, December 28, 1984.

Hilberg, Raul. "Conscience from Burlington." *Hadassah Magazine.* August/September, 1991.

The Holocaust in Contemporary Art. Exhibit at the Holman Hall Art Gallery, March 27-April 15, 1989. Trenton: Trenton State College, 1989.

Hunter, Sam. *Larry Rivers.* New York: Rizzoli, 1989.

Kampf, Avram. *Jewish Experience in the Art of the Twentieth Century.* South Hadley: Bergin and Garvey, 1984.

Kiefer, Anselm. *The Books of Anselm Kiefer, 1969-1990.* New York: Braziller, 1991.

Kitaj, R.B. *First Diaspora Manifesto by R.B. Kitaj.* London: Thames and Hudson, 1989.

Kushner, Marilyn. "Holocaust Art Is Testimony, not Art." *Shema, A Journal of Jewish Responsibility.* No. 15/284, December 28, 1984.

Lasansky, Mauricio. *The Nazi Drawings by Mauricio Lasansky.* Iowa City: University of Iowa Press, 1976.

Liss, Andrea. *Trespassing Through Shadows: Memory, Photography, and the Holocaust.* Visible Evidence Series, Vol. 3. Minneapolis: University of Minnesota Press, 1998.

Makarova, Elena. *From Bauhaus to Terezin: Freidl Dickler-Brandeis and Her Pupils.* Jerusalem: Yad VaShem, 1990.

Milton, Sybil. *In Fitting Memory: The Art and Politics of Holocaust Memorials.* Detroit: Wayne State University Press, 1992.

_____. *The Story of Karl Stojka: A Childhood in* Birkenau. Exhibition at the Embassy of Austria. Washington: US Holocaust Commission, l992.

Morrison, Paul and Hannah Rothschild (Producers). *From Bitter Earth: Artists and the Holocaust.* London: BBC and Omnibus Co., l988. Distributed through TVI Ltd, l42 Wardover Street, London.

Novitch, Miriam and Lucy Davidowicz. *Art from the Concentration Camps, l940-l945.* Philadelphia: Jewish Publication Society, l98l.

Oppler, Ellen C. *Rico LeBrun: Tranformations/Transfiguration.* Syracuse: Syracuse University School of Art, l983.

Rothschild-Boros, Monica C. *In the Shadow of the Tower: The Works of Josef Nassy, l942-l945.* Irvine: Severin Wunderman Museum, l989.

Saloman, Charlotte. *Charlotte: A Diary in Pictures.* New York: Harcourt, l963.

_____. *Life or Theatre. An Autobiographical Play by Charlotte Saloman.* New York: Viking Press, l98l.

Salmon-Livine, Irit. *Testimony Art of the Holocaust.* Jerusalem: Yad VaShem, 1986.

Seeing Through Paradise: Artists in the Terezin Concentration Camp. Boston: Exhibition at the Massachusetts College of Art, March 6—May 4, l991.

Semin, Didier. *Boltanski.* New York: Art Press, l988.

Spiritual Resistance: Art from the Concentration Camps, l940-45. Philadelphia: Jewish Publication Society, l98l.

Terna, Fred. "Reflections of a Survivor/Artist." *Shema, a Journal of Jewish Responsibility.* No. l5/284, December 28, l984.

Thompson, Vivian Alpert. *A Mission in Art.* Macon: Mercer University Press, 1988.

Toll, Nellie S. *Behind the Secret Window: A Memoir of a Hidden Childhood during World War II.* New York: Dial, l992.

Van Alphen, Ernst. *Caught by History: Holocaust Effects in Contemporary Art, Literature and Theory.* Stanford: Stanford University Press, 1998.

Witkin, Jerome. *West '85: Art and the Law.* St. Paul: West Publishing, l985.

Witnesses in the Anteroom to Hell: The Theresienstadt Drawings of Paul Schwartz and Leo Lowit. South Yaria, Victoria: The Jewish Museum of Australia, l990.

Young, James T. *The Texture of Memory.* New Haven: Yale University Press, 1993.

_____.(Ed.) *The Art of Memory: Holocaust Memorials in History.* New York and Munich: Prestel-Verlag, 1994.

_____. *At Memory's Edge: After-Images of the Holocaust in Contemporary Art and Architecture.* New Haven: Yale University Press, 2000.

Zelizer, Barbie. *Remembering to Forget: Holocaust Memory Through the Camera's Eye.* Chicago: University of Chicago Press, 1998.

_____.(Ed.) *Visual Culture and the Holocaust.* New Brunswick: Rutgers University Press, 2000.

FRITZ HIRSCHBERGER

THE SUR-RATIONAL
HOLOCAUST
PAINTINGS

The Same Fire
(oil and collage on canvas, 52" x 36")

Melting the tallow heretics
Ousting the Jews
Their thick palls flow

Over the cicatrix of Poland, burnt-out
Germany
They do not die.

Grey birds obsess my heart,
Mouth-ash, of eye,
They settle. On the high

Precipice
That emptied one man into space
The ovens glowed like heavens? Incandescent

It is a heart,
This holocaust I walk in,
O golden child the world will kill and eat.

(from *Mary's Son,* by Sylvia Plath)

Let us Pray for the Perfidious Jews
or Nulla Salus Extra Ecclesiam
(No Salvation Outside the Church)
(oil on canvas, 60" x 40")

The first part of the title is taken from a prayer that was part of the Roman Catholic liturgy until it was rescinded by Vatican II. In 1984 a small group of Carmelite nuns established a convent at Auschwitz Concentration Camp in a building that had stored Zyklon B, the prussic acid used in the gas chambers to exterminate the victims of the Nazis. In addition, the nuns erected a huge cross in front of the building. The nuns believed that praying over the dead would hasten the return of their souls to Jesus. It is morbid and ironic that when the 1,500,000 Jews were murdered at Auschwitz the ones who now want to rob the souls of the murdered Jews were silent.

Despite an agreement reached in 1987 between the European Jewish Congress and the Cardinals of Lyon, Brussels, and Poland to relocate them, the nuns refused to move. In February 1990, ground was broken to build an interfaith center outside the camp to settle the dispute between the Polish Catholic Church and the international Jewish organizations.

Though the nuns have been removed, the site of Auschwitz continues to be the center of struggle between Polish and Jewish memory of victimization.

The Concordat
(oil on canvas, 54" x 48")

On July 8th, 1933, the year Hitler came to power in Germany, the Vatican signed an agreement (the Concordat) with Hitler, by which the Nazi government promised to respect Roman Catholic rights, practices and institutions in Nazi Germany. In return, the Vatican and the German Catholic clergy were supposed to support the authoritarian and nationalist stances of the Third Reich. By 1938 the Vatican understood that the Concordat had helped solidify Nazi power.

Many events relating to Jewish destruction happened virtually in front of the Vatican. During Fall 1943, 8,000 Jews were rounded up in Rome. The Pope agreed to help Jews with ransom of gold if necessary. The ransom amount, however, was raised by the Jews. On October 18, 1943, 1,007 Roman Jews were rounded up and sent to Auschwitz. The Pope remained silent, except for the intervention on behalf of 2 Jews. 7,000 went into hiding and survived; 4,000 were hidden with the knowledge and the approval of the Pope.

During the war, the Church encouraged the rescue of Jews; it offered money and, occasionally, facilities. But the main burden of rescue fell on individual Christians, rather than on the institution.

Zyklon B
(oil on canvas, 45" x 34")

Shamefully
the blue
fills rooms
with death color,
it swirls
amethyst-crystals
to paint
death onto
canvas
forgetting the blue
of the sea
to pour death
through sky
to take away
breath,
deceiving with the
most beautiful
of blues,
raining death
blue.

(Alice Rogoff, San Francisco, 1991)

Zyklon B, prussic acid in the form of amethyst-colored crystals, was used in Auschwitz and other extermination camps to murder by gassing the victims of the Nazis. The crystals were dropped through openings in the ceiling of the gas chambers. To fool the victims and to avoid panic, the gas chambers were disguised with fake shower heads to look like regular showers.

I.G. Farben, which made Zyklon B, also owned Bayer A.G., the parent company of Bayer Aspirin. Farben still exists and owns Bayer, BASF and Hoetsch.

Indifference
(oil on canvas, 60" x 48")

Fear not your enemies, for they can only kill you.
Fear not your friends, for they can only betray you.
Fear only the indifferent, who permit the killers
and betrayers to walk safely on earth.

(Edward Yashinski, Yiddish poet who survived the Shoah only to die in a communist prison in Poland.)

The Hypocritical Oath
(oil on canvas, 40" x 60")

The Nazi Doctors, 50% of all the doctors in Germany by 1944, did not take the Hippocratic oath, but swore allegiance to the Reich and to the protection of Aryan blood. Many became involved in medical experiments on concentration camp inmates. The selection of the inmates for the gas chambers was also performed by medical doctors.

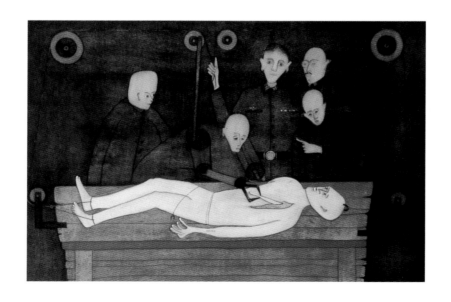

Darkness U. S. A.

(oil on canvas, 60" x 40")

On January 21, 1943, the Polish Jewish National Committee (ZKN), the political arm of the Polish Jewish Combat Organization ZOB, sent a radio message to New York addressed to Stephen Wise of the American Jewish Congress, Nahum Goldman of the World Jewish Congress, and to George Bocker of the Joint Distribution Committee. It notified them of "the greatest crime of all times, about the murder of millions of Jews in Poland. Poised on the brink of annihilation of the still surviving Jews, we ask you for:

1. Revenge against the Germans.
2. Force the Hitlerites to halt the murder.
3. Fight for our lives and our honor.
4. Contact the neutral countries.
5. Rescue 10,000 children through exchange.
6. 500,000 dollars for purposes of aid.

Brothers—the remaining Jews in Poland live with the awareness that in the most terrible days of our history you did not come to our aid. Respond at least in the last days of our life."

At 6 a.m. on Passover eve, April 19, 1943, the "last days" began for the Warsaw Jewry as heavily armed SS troops started the total annihilation of the Warsaw ghetto.

Semper Idem
(Always the Same)
(oil on canvas, 54" x 40")

Poland, 1946. After the defeat of the Nazis, over 1,000 Jews, survivors of the Nazi death camps, were murdered by Poles when they returned to their homes, while the Polish Security Police and clergy stood idly by. After the Shoah, in June 1946, the Jewish population of Poland was 240,489. In July 1946, when the pogroms against the Jews in Poland reached their most serious point, about 150,000 terror-stricken Jews fled Poland. The remaining Jews, about 80,000, became scapegoats of the 1967 and 1969 anti-Jewish terror campaign orchestrated by the ruling communist government. As a result, most Jews were forced to leave Poland. Thus, after living un-interrupted for 1000 years in Poland, through the combined effort of the Nazis, the Poles and the communists, the Jewish population of Poland was reduced from over 3,200,000 in 1939 to less than 8,000 at the end of the century.

Deutsche Kammermusik
(German "Chamber" Music)
(oil on canvas, 54" x 40")

At the Auschwitz/Birkenau extermination camp, some of the world's finest musicians were forced to perform for the amusement of the Nazi SS guards, while their Jewish victims were tortured and gassed. Henry Meyer, Gisela Hirschberger's cousin, played the violin in one of the death camp orchestras at Auschwitz/Birkenau. He survived and became a protégé of Isaac Stern. Henry Meyer and three other survivors of the Shoah founded the world famous *La Salle* string quartet.

The Children's Home at Jozefinska Street, Krakow, Poland
(oil on canvas, 48" x 36")

One of the cruelest stories of the Holocaust is the deportation of orphans. This took place in nearly every country, but the best-known stories are the deportations from France and from the Polish cities of Krakow and Warsaw.

"At Jozefinska Street, the Germans started to liquidate the *Kinderheim* ('home for children'). Wagons arrived into which the children were loaded. The small ones were thrown into baskets and carried to the wagons, several at a time. The older were led to the square and shot at the corner of the blind alley."

(from the book *The Krakow Ghetto Pharmacy* by Tadeusz Pankiewicz. The author is a Polish gentile pharmacist who owned and operated a pharmacy in the ghetto, and an eyewitness to the murder of the children.)

**Two Jewish Mothers
or The Law of Unintended Consequence**
(oil on canvas, 60" x 40")

The Law of Unintended Consequence relates to the question of the consequences of the Virgin Birth and the Ministry of Jesus, rejected by the Jews and made by Paul of Tarsus into Christianity. Christianity became a major force for demonizing Jews during the Middle Ages. Was Christianity part of the Holocaust? Scholars believe that Christianity did not cause the Holocaust, but the selection of Jews as victims could not have been done without the long history of Christian Contra-Judaic views. A simple question: If Jesus had not been born, would the Holocaust have been avoided? If Jesus had been born in 1943, would he have died at Auschwitz?

Martyr Number 44074
(oil on canvas, 60" x 40")

Born a Jew, Edith Stein converted to Catholicism and became a nun before Hitler assumed power in Germany. She lived as a Catholic; yet she died in 1942, during the time of the Concordat, in an Auschwitz gas chamber as Jew number 44074. In 1987, Catholic again, Pope John Paul II elevated Edith Stein to Martyr Benedicta of the Cross, the first step toward sainthood.

The Last Lesson
(oil on canvas, 48" x 36")

A Nazi guard talking to a nine-year-old Jewish boy who is on his way to be gassed in an Auschwitz gas chamber:

"Well, my boy, you know a lot for your age."

"I know that I know a lot, and I also know
that I won't learn any more," the boy replies.

(from the sworn testimony of witness Wolken; the 1965 trial of Nazi criminals, Frankfurt am Main, Germany.)

Ein Deutsches Wiegenlied
(A German Lullaby)
(oil on canvas, 54" x 36")

The visual text of the painting relates to an event reported in Auschwitz, a report of the proceedings against Robert Karl Ludwig Mulka and other 20 members of the SS administration at Auschwitz, in Frankfurt am Main, December 20, 1963. In February 1943, during one morning, a group of 30 to 40 children arrived from Zamosc, a small town in Poland, to the Auschwitz camp. They were allowed to play in Block 20. In the afternoon, an order was given to kill the children. They were led into the washrooms, told to undress and were murdered with Phenol injections into the heart by SS Medical orderlies Scherpe and Hantl. Klodinski, a witness, recalled that all he heard were thumps of the children's bodies falling against the floor. Scherpe was sentenced to 4 years and 6 months hard labor, Hantl to 3 years.

Herr Landau Comes Home
(oil on canvas, 48" x 36")

Arrested in September 1939 in Hamburg, Germany, by the Nazis, Mr. Landau was shipped to the notorious concentration camp Dachau, located in Bavaria, about 15 km northwest of Munich. In 1941, Mr. Landau was murdered and cremated by the SS camp guards. His ashes, in a cigar box, were delivered by an official of the Gestapo (the Secret State Police) to the home of the Landau family in Hamburg. There, he threw the cigar box on the kitchen table in front of Mrs. Landau and her daughters, 11-year-old Karin and 16-year-old Cecille. When asked about the meaning of the box, the Gestapo man's cynical reply was: "Mr. Landau!"

Mrs. Sala Landau died of starvation in the Lodz ghetto. Karin was murdered by the Nazis. Cecille miraculously survived the Shoah.

(from the German edition of the book *Von Asche zum Leben*, published in 1992. Author: Lucille Eichengreen, née Cecille Landau. The English edition, *From Ashes to Life* has been published by Mercury Press, San Francisco, 1992.)

The Fifth Horseman
(oil on canvas, 60" x 48")

For every evil under the sun
There is a remedy or none.
If there be one, seek till you find it;
If there be none, never mind it.

(*Mother Goose*)

The Book of Revelations of the Christian Bible tells the story of the Four Horsemen of the Apocalypse. They symbolize the four elements of destruction: Famine, Pestilence, War, and Death. The four horses are white, red, black, and pale. The name of the Fifth Horseman is said to be Hades or Hell. The Fifth Horseman operates in the shadow of the Fourth. It was common belief, especially during the Reformation, that one could not defend oneself or one's faith against those things that one was unable to discern with one's physical senses. The war predicted to be waged by the Fifth Horseman will occur on a different plane. It is a plane that the physical senses are not able to discern. And despite this apparent handicap, the Fifth Horseman will not have pity or mercy on his victims.

Zyklon B, or Prussic Acid, was used at Auschwitz and Maidanek death camps. The B in Zyklon B stood for the blue color it had when going through chemical change, which, according to scholars, left some blue discoloring on the walls of the gas chambers. Under the horse's feet are the names of the death camps where this gas as well as carbon monoxide were used.

The famous *The Four Horsemen of the Apocalypse* is an engraving by the German Renaissance artist Albrecht Dürer, who lived in Nuremberg, the same city that gave rise to the Nazi rallies during 1933 and 1934.

The Seduction of Germania
(oil on canvas, 54" x 36")

The making of Hitler and the seduction of Germania were the direct results of the harsh conditions of the 1919 Treaty of Versailles, imposed on Germany on the insistence of a vengeful France. Hitler blamed all the ills that befell the Weimar Republic in 1922, 1923 and again in 1929 on the punishing conditions of the Treaty of Versailles. He promised to abrogate the terms of the Treaty of Versailles, to restore Germany's national pride, blaming the Jews for the defeat of Germany by using the canard of the "Stab in the Back!" He promised restoration of the economy and an end to unemployment. His rhetoric resulted in large electoral gains, but the Nazis never gained an electoral majority. Only disunity among the opposing parties made the appointment of Hitler as chancellor in 1933 possible.

Germania is the ancient name for the area inhabited by the Germanic tribes, as described by the Roman historian Tacitus in his book, *Germania*. Tacitus noted the following about the German people:

The Inhabitants. Origins of the Name Germany. "The Germans themselves I should regard as aboriginal and not mixed at all with other races through immigration or intercourse. In their ancient songs, their only way of remembering or recording the past was to celebrate an earth-born god, Tuisco, and his son, Mannus, as the origin of their race, as their founders… The name Germany, on the other hand, they say is modern and newly introduced, from the fact that the tribes which first crossed the Rhine and drove out the Gauls, and are now called Tungrians, were then called Germans. Thus what was the name of a tribe, and not of a race, gradually prevailed."

Physical Characteristics. "I agree with those who think that the tribes of Germany are free from all taint of intermarriages with foreign nations, and that they appear as a distinct, unmixed race, like none but themselves. Hence, too, the same physical peculiarities throughout so vast a population. All have fierce blue eyes, red hair, huge frames, fit only for a sudden exertion. They are less able to bear laborious work. Heat and thirst they cannot in the least endure; to cold and hunger their climate and their soil inure them."

On Women and Warfare. "Tradition says that armies already wavering and giving way have been rallied by women who, with earnest entreaties and bosoms laid bare, have vividly represented the horrors of captivity, which the Germans fear with such extreme dread on behalf of their women, that the strongest tie by which a state can be bound is that of being required to give, among the number of hostages, maidens of noble birth. They even believe that the sex has a certain sanctity and prescience, and they do not despise their counsels, or make light of their answers. In Vespasian's days, we saw Veleda, long regarded by many as a divinity. In former times, too, they venerated Aurinia, and many other women, but not with servile flatteries, or with sham deification."

The Double Cross

(oil and collage on canvas, 36" x 36")

The hooked cross (swastika), placed in the center of the traditional symbol of Christianity, was adapted by the protestant *German Christian Movement* (*Deutsche Christen*, or short, D.C.) as their symbol. As a group within the German Protestant Church, it was openly endorsed by the Nazi party. In 1933 they dominated the unifying process of the 29 regional churches into the Protestant Reich Church. The Deutsche Christen managed to get Ludwig Müller, their own man, elected Reich bishop. Here is one of their credos:

"Because in the course of historical development, corrupting Jewish influence has also been active in Christianity, the de-Judaization of the Church and of Christianity has become the inescapable and decisive duty of the Church today; it is the requirement for the future of Christianity."

Originally, the swastika was a symbol that came from India; it still can be found in abundance in the Hindu culture, mainly meaning good luck. Hitler took the symbol, which is believed to have been part of the carvings in the Catholic Church he attended in Linz, Austria, and reversed the orientation of the hooks. He made it look more dynamic, suggesting a circular move from left to right. This transformed swastika became the symbol of his political party—NSDAP—The Nazi Party. Other scholars have recalled it is a variant of a Greek cross, found in many decorative elements before the twentieth century.

After 1933, the German Christian Movement displayed the traditional cross with a Swastika at the point of crossing, with a D and a C, symbolizing the name of the Church. In 1938, NSDAP came out with new versions of the Bible and with biographies of Christ the Aryan, which attempted to eradicate the Judaic roots of Christianity. De-Judaization of the Christian church was considered a goal of all Party members and the Churches.

Charlie Chaplin's 1940 American film *The Great Dictator* used the symbol of "the double cross" for the flag of the Hitler look-alike. The English meaning of the word double cross relates to the treachery of the Nazis and the false promises that ultimately led to the destruction of Germany as well as of its victims.

The Yekkes
(Yiddish word for German Jews)
(oil on canvas, 48" x 36")

We have lived here in believing
What we were taught:
That things consist in their consistency
And we have built on this foundation
A castle of playing cards
With the appearance of appearances
With shadows of shadows.

(Miguel de Unamuno)

Jews had lived for hundreds of years in Germany, making tremendous contributions to German science, industry, economy, and arts. During World War I, they fought valiantly for their *Vaterland*, many decorated with the coveted Iron Cross First Class. Yet from one day to another they were deprived of their nationality and citizenship.

Yekkes is a term describing Jews who adopted the snobbish German Jewish cultural values defying the fraditional Jewish identity. They were contemptuous of those they called *Ostjuden*, small-town (shtetl) Jews from Eastern Europe and were blind toward the Nazi threat. The name *Yekkes* came "possibly because they always wore a jacket, *jacke*... The appelation *Yekke* was soon applied to anyone who was thorough, punctual and polite." (Meir Ronnen, "Last of His Kind," *The Jerusalem Post*, December 9, 2001). However, German Jews, who were highly assimilated into German society, found themselves being identified by racial laws in the 1930s, culminating in the Law for the Protection of German Honor of September 15, 1935. This law defined a Jew as anyone with three or four Jewish grandparents, irrespective of their current religious affiliation.

After the rise of the Nazis to power in 1933, even Jewish men who had served in the Imperial German Army of World War I were accused of illegally earning medals and were given only a temporary respite from deportation.

44

The Price for Silence
or "The Chickens Always Come Home to Roost"
(oil on canvas, 48" x 36")

The "price for silence" is the loss of one's own rights. One of the best commentaries on this was by Martin Niemoller (1892-1984):

First they came for the Communists,
 and I didn't speak up,
  because I wasn't a Communist.
Then they came for the Jews,
 and I didn't speak up,
  because I wasn't a Jew.
Then they came for the Catholics,
 and I didn't speak up,
  because I was a Protestant.
Then they came for me,
 and by that time there was no one
  left to speak up for me.

Niemoller declared that he "would rather burn his church to the ground, than preach the Nazi trinity of 'race, blood, and soil.'"

Niemoller, however, also was tainted. He had been a U-boat captain in WW I, prior to becoming a pastor, and he supported Hitler prior to his taking power. Indeed, initially the Nazi press held him up as a model for his service in WW I. Niemoller broke very early with the Nazis. In 1933, he organized the Pastor's Emergency League to protect Lutheran pastors from the police. In 1934, he was one of the leading organizers at the Barmen Synod and Declaration, which produced the theological basis for the Confessing Church, an enduring symbol of German resistance to Hitler. At one point he declared that it was impossible to "point to the German [Luther] without pointing to the Jew [Christ] to which he pointed to." (from Charles Colson, *Kingdoms in Conflict*)

Rev. Martin Niemoller was protected until 1937 both by the foreign press and by influential friends in the up-scale Berlin suburb where he preached. Eventually, he was arrested for treason and found guilty. Perhaps due to foreign pressure, he was initially given only a suspended sentence. He was however then almost immediately re-arrested on Hitler's direct orders. From then on until the end of WW II, he was held at the Sachsenhausen and Dachau concentration camps. Near the end of the war, he narrowly escaped execution.

The Saint Louis Blues
(oil and collage on canvas, 54" x 36")

On May 13, 1939, 930 Jews with legal landing permits left Hamburg on the German liner St. Louis for Havana, Cuba. On arrival they were told to pay an additional $500 bond per person to guarantee they would not become welfare clients, or entry to Cuba would be denied. The destitute Jews begged the U.S. Jewish Joint Distribution Committee to save them. They refused. So did the U.S. Department of State, by not permitting the refugees from Nazi terror to land in Florida. Returned to Europe, some escaped extermination, others perished in the Nazi death camps. In 1937 Rabbi Stephen Wise wrote to a New York congressman, who intended to introduce legislation to ease the restrictions on immigration:

"I wish I thought it were possible for this measure to be passed without repercussions upon the Jewish community in this country. I have every reason to believe, unfortunately, that any effort that is made at this time to waive the immigration laws will result in a serious accentuation of what we know to be a rising wave of anti-Semitic feeling in this country." (from Rafael Medoff, *The Deadening Silence*)

Manuel Benitez, Cuban Minister of Immigration, was a major player in the fate of the refugees since it was he who had signed their landing permits. Benitez maintained that President Bru of Cuba would back down since the St. Louis was allowed in the harbor. He wanted $250,000 in bribes so that he could try to amend his relations with Bru and rescind Decree 937 that discriminated against refugees. President Bru refused to listen to Benitez' requests. Though he no longer had access to Bru, he continued to espouse his assurance that Bru would back down. His confident attitude convinced a number of influential people that the circumstances were not as serious as they seemed, thus action was not taken.

The St. Louis was forced to return to Europe in June 1939. However, Great Britain, France, Belgium, and the Netherlands agreed to accept the stranded refugees. After German forces occupied Western Europe in 1940, many St. Louis passengers and other Jewish refugees who had entered those countries were caught up in the Final Solution, the Nazi plan to murder the Jews of Europe.

The Abandonment of the Marranos
(oil on canvas, 48" x 36")

With the arrival of Hitler, Jews that had converted to Christianity, many before the turn of the century, were without any real resistance, abandoned by their churches to the terror of Nazi persecution and death in concentration camps.

Marrano was a derogatory term used to describe Jews who converted to Christianity in 14th and 15th century Spain. After the riots of 1381, there were many forced conversions. However, after the period of difficulty was over, many of these converts did not return to Judaism, but found they had greater mobility in society as "New Christians." The Spain of Ferdinand and Isabella was nonetheless determined to rid the country of Judaizing tendencies.The Spanish Jews were expelled in 1492, but the Marranos, now Catholics, were accused of secretly practicing Judaism, an act which made them heretics. Most of them were tried by the Spanish Inquisition and killed by burning.

The Nazi law undercut the Christian concept of mission to the Jews. Possibly, this may have been the first step in ultimately destroying Christianity, for, after all, Christianity was Judaic. Hirschberger's image is derived from the medieval scenes of the Martyrdom of Saint Sebastian. Sebastian is an ideal model for the Marrano theme. He was a soldier in the Roman army and performed so well that the emperor Diocletian made him a captain without ever guessing Sebastian was a Christian. As more and more Christians died, it was inevitable that Sebastian would be found out. Diocletian was furious at what he saw as a betrayal after all he had done for Sebastian. He ordered Sebastian to be shot by archers.

The Way of All My Flesh
The Stigma of Fragments of Memory
(oil on canvas, 54" x 40")

The scene juxtaposes two images. In the foreground, there is a survivor in old age, holding a toy that evokes the images, fragments of memory, of those in his family, particularly children, who have been lost during the Holocaust. In the background, a woman with a child, possibly his wife, is going into the gas chambers, which were routinely labeled "showers."

Why Did Birds Not of a Feather Flock Together?
(oil on canvas, 32" x 40")

The title of this painting comes from an old German song whose lyrics read:

Birds of a feather flock together,
And so will pigs and swine;
Rats and mice
Will have their choice,
And so will I have mine.

This painting is reminiscent of *The Bark of Dante* or *Dante and Virgil in Hell* by Eugene Delacroix. This famous 19th century Romantic painting was inspired by Dante's *Inferno*. There, the red-robed Latin poet Virgil guides Dante through Hell, where the demonic souls of the Florentines try to get into the boat as it crosses the River Styx.

The Last Family Outing. Destination Kulmhof
(oil on canvas, 48" x 30")

Kulmhof or Chelmno, located in Poland, was the first Nazi extermination camp. After the victims' arrival at Chelmno, they were taken in groups of fifty—men, women and children—to the ground floor of the Schloss, the castle. There they were told to strip and put their valuables in a basket. The victims were then taken to the cellar past signs reading "To the Washroom." From there, they were brought to an enclosed ramp. At the end of the ramp stood a gas van with its doors open. The moment the victims entered the ramp, the Nazis forced them with blows to run into the van.

The gas vans were supplied to the Einsatzgruppen and to the Chelmno death camps in November-December 1941. The killing in Chelmno began on December 8, 1941. When the van returned to the camp after a drive in the countryside, the dead or half-dead bodies were thrown into furnaces. Chelmno became operative in November 1941, and continued to operate until January 1945. Approximately 320,000 victims were killed there. There were only three survivors from this camp. Gas vans were used in the murder of approximately 700,000 people throughout Nazi-dominated Europe.

Chelmno was the first extermination camp that experimented with mobile gas chambers. These were large vans produced by Dodge, Mercedes and Saurer, modified so that the exhaust fumes came into the cargo area and asphyxiated the victims. Two types of gas vans were built: a larger one, 5.8 meters in length, and a smaller one, measuring 4.5 meters. Both were about 2.5 meters wide and 1.7 meters high. The bigger one could accommodate between 130 and 150 people, when densely packed inside, and the smaller one from 80 to 100.

No Exit

(oil on canvas, 48" x 30")

Some German Jews informed of their deportation could not face the trial and committed suicide. In Mannheim, out of 2,500 deportees, 10 committed suicide. In Baden-Baden, with scarcely 100 community members, 10 killed themselves. More suicides occurred during their transport to an unknown, to them, destination. Most of these cases of suicide involved almost exclusively German Jews, who had moved away from Judaism, or had been baptized, or had become atheists. The Nuremberg Laws, issued in September 1935, returned them to Judaism, they who had not wanted to be Jews.

Between 1933 and 1939 almost half of Germany's Jews left the country, reducing the Jewish population from 500,000 to about 300,000. However, among those 300,000 who stayed in Germany until Jewish emigration was banned in 1941, the basic hope remained that the situation would improve. When Jewish schools were closed, they organized clandestine classes. When university courses were closed to Jewish students, banned Jewish professors lectured in secret. When synagogues were closed, prayer groups sprang up in private homes and basements.

Suicides, however, rose as the true nature of Nazi race policy presented itself and increased markedly after November 9/10, 1938, the Kristallnacht in Germany and Austria. There were ten recorded suicides in Nuremberg on November 10. In Vienna, an estimated 47,000 of the city's 176,000 Jewish population was reduced to poverty. Four months after the Anschluss, the number of Jewish suicides in Vienna alone was computed as about 7,000. The German-Jewish suicide rate in the 1930s was the highest in the world.

A Willing Collaborator
(oil on canvas, 54" x 36")

Chaim Mordechai Rumkowski was the Nazi appointed dictatorial chairman of the *Judenrat* (Jewish Council) of the Lodz-Litzmannstadt Ghetto, Poland. Ghetto population, April 30, 1940, approximately 164,000.

In 1942, Rumkowski complied with the demand of the Nazis to hand over all children under 10 years of age, all Jews over 65 and the infirm to the Nazis for deportation (extermination). A combined total of 24,000. In a compassionate speech to the mothers of the Lodz Ghetto, Rumkowski begged them to hand over their children. The mothers refused. Subsequently, in a brutal round-up, 20,000 souls were collected and sent to be murdered in extermination camps. Rumkowski asked the Council of Rabbis to participate in the deportation selection process. They refused.

Maimonides in his *Yessoday Ha Torah*, citing *Mishna Trumot* 12:8, concludes that Jews cannot hand over even one Jew to the enemy to save their own lives. Adam Czerniakow, the elder of the Warsaw Ghetto, was ordered by the Nazis in 1942 to provide a daily quota of 3,000 Jews, the quota had also to include children. Rather than collaborate with the Nazis, he committed suicide on July 23, 1942.

Rumkowski spent much energy appeasing German demands, and, in this process, he set up a near-dictatorship within his "ghetto kingdom." The Lodz Ghetto became practically a starving slave colony, a grotesque replica of society with "classes" of the "haves and have-nots," and where being "connected" could keep one from being deported, or could allow one to obtain extra food or secure an administrative job—not unlike the "organizing" that was required for survival in concentration camps. He zealously "organized" the ghetto to satisfy the demands of the Germans for order as well as quotas for deportation. He thought that he could insure survival of himself and some part of the ghetto population by producing war-goods for the German Army. He established food rationing to control the starving masses as the need arose. He set up a complex internal "government" complete with his own infamous "Jewish Police" and deportation department (i.e., Office for Resettled Persons).

From Rumkowski's speech (September 4, 1942): "A grievous blow has struck the ghetto. They are asking us to give up the best we possess—the children and the elderly. I was unworthy of having a child of my own, so I gave the best years of my life to children. I've lived and breathed with children, I never imagined I would be forced to deliver this sacrifice to the altar with my own hands. In my old age, I must stretch out my hands and beg: Brothers and sisters! Hand them over to me! Fathers and mothers: Give me your children!"

April 19, 1943. The Day the Gods Went to Lunch and Never Came Back
(oil on canvas, 47" x 36")

On April 19, 1943, the destruction of the Warsaw Ghetto began. The remaining Jewish population, depleted by transports to the death camp at Treblinka, was exterminated. Units of SS stormed the Ghetto under the command of General Stroop. Unexpectedly, Jewish resistance was strong, and it took more than a month for the Germans to subdue the Warsaw Ghetto.

Four weeks later, on May 16, 1943, SS Major General and Major General of the (German State) police Stroop made the following announcement: "The Jewish Quarter of Warsaw is no more!" 56,065 Jewish survivors of the ghetto were sent to concentration or death camps. Many of those who survived immigrated to Palestine after the war and established Lochemai Hagedaot, The Warsaw Ghetto Fighter's Kibbutz, north of Haifa, now Israel. With some irony, on the same day the extermination of the Warsaw Ghetto began, April 19, 1943, representatives of the United States and Great Britain met in Bermuda to seek a solution to the refugee problem. As at Evian in 1938, no solution was found.

The title of this painting suggests some theological problems. God and the Jewish people have always been seen together. The artist's title suggests the absence of God during the Uprising, as well as the Holocaust. In this painting, the image of a Jewish martyr appears on the right with a "Jewish" halo in the form of a Star of David. His right hand is raised in the form of a Jewish sacramental blessing of the Hebrew letter shin, one of the symbols of the name of God. But this gesture is incomplete, as the usual symbol is two fingers separated from the next two fingers, and the thumb, forming in Latin letters what looks like a W.

Theologians have debated the question raised here. One answer is that God gave man free will. Therefore, according to theologian Franklin Sherman, man is free to create gas chambers and use them. On the other side are the commandments, the 6th of which is "Thou shalt not commit murder."

The Fish Had No Legs
A Quorum without a Prayer
A Shower without Water
(oil on canvas, 48" x 36")

The Catholic Church failed to honor the legacy of Saint Peter, the First Pope. Pope Pius XII resisted to intercede for the Jews because of his fear of communism. The "Quorum," or "minyan" in Hebrew, refers to the ten men or Jews necessary for prayer to commence. The Jewish faith system also failed during the Holocaust. The Nazi perpetrators usually disguised gas chambers as showers and labeled them "Brausebad."

The debate about Pope Pius XII continues. Only the opening of the Vatican's archives could end the debate of this institution's war and post-war politics.

SS Gymnastics
(oil on canvas, 48" x 36")

This painting is based on a story the artist read about several years ago. On April 20, 1945, seventeen days before the end of World War II in Europe, a truck from the Neuengamme concentration camp near Hamburg delivered twenty two Jewish children, between the ages of four and twelve, to the empty school on Bullenhuser Damm in the northern part of the city. All the children had survived medical experiments in Auschwitz. The SS knew that—alive—these children constituted a proof of the Nazi crimes. On the same April afternoon, the children were taken into the large gym and hanged. The story was not made public until 1988, when information appeared in Lea Rosh's documentary, which was not shown to English speaking audiences. A former talk show host, Rosh created the documentary *Der Tod ist ein Meister aus Deutschland* (Death is a Master from Germany) with Eberhard Jackel.

Arts and Crafts in the Third Reich
(oil on canvas, 48" x 48")

Ilse Koch ("The Bitch of Buchenwald"), the wife of concentration camp commander Karl Otto Koch, shared her husband's hobby of collecting patches of tattooed human skin and shrunken human heads. It was she who selected the living persons with the interesting tattoos whose skin she wanted. After they were killed, she had them skinned and used the tattooed patches of skin to fashion lampshades. The issues raised may seem macabre, but they reflect back on body parts taken by conquerors in other times and places from their victims—more recently, in the 1990's, during the Bosnian war. This was true on both sides in the American frontier experience, as well as in other acts of genocide. Ilse Koch was first released, then re-arrested by the Allied Control forces, and sentenced to life imprisonment. She committed suicide in 1967.

Dr. Wagner, who wrote a doctoral dissertation on tattooing, had the entire camp searched for people with tattoos, and had them photographed. The prisoners were later called to the gate by Commandant Koch, selected according to the splendor of their tattooed skin, and sent into the infirmary. Soon thereafter the best examples of skin appeared in the pathology department, where they were prepared and shown, for years, to SS visitors as special treasures. Koch had an "artistic" table lamp made for him out of human bones, stretched over with human skin. Hundreds of prepared human skins were sent to Berlin on orders of the chief doctor for the concentration camps, SS Colonel Dr. Lolling.

The fact that Koch had lamps made of human skin, which of course had to be decorated with "artistic" tattoos, did not distinguish him from the other SS officers: they had the same "artworks" made for their family homes. It is more interesting that Frau Koch had a lady's handbag made out of the same material. She was just as proud of it as a South Sea island woman would have been about her cannibal trophies.

(from *The Buchenwald Report,* translated and edited by David A. Hackett)

65

Zegota
(oil on canvas, 60" x 36")

Code name of *Rada Pomocy Zydom* (Council for Aid to Jews), an underground organization in occupied Poland, Zegota was in operation from December 1942 until the liberation of Poland in January 1945. It was preceded by the *Tymczasowy Komitet Pomocy Zydom* (Provisional Committee for Aid to Jews), founded on September 27, 1942, on the initiative of Zofia Kossak-Szczucka, who also became its chairperson. Made up of democratic Catholic activists, the Provisional Committee had 180 persons under its care. On December 4, 1942, it became Zegota. Zegota had on its board representatives of five Polish and two Jewish political movements.

Concealing Jews was punishable in Poland by death for all the persons living in the house where they were discovered. A difficult problem therefore was to find hiding places for persons who looked Jewish. Zegota was on a constant lookout for suitable accommodations. No estimate can be given of the magnitude of this form of aid by Zegota, but it appears to have been great. Children were put in the care of foster families, into public orphanages, or similar institutions maintained by convents. The foster families were told that the children were relatives, distant or close, and they were paid by Zegota for the children's maintenance. In Warsaw, Zegota had twenty five hundred children registered whom it looked after in this way. Medical attention for the Jews in hiding was also made available. Zegota had ties with many ghettos and camps. It also made numerous efforts to induce the Polish government in exile and the Delegatura to appeal to the Polish population to help the persecuted Jews.

During the war, Zegota was the only rescue organization that was run jointly by Jews and non-Jews, and its adherents came from a wide range of political movements. Zegota was the only organization that, despite the arrests of some of its members, was able to operate for a considerable length of time and to extend help to Jews in so many different ways.

Members of Zegota were memorialized in Israel on October 28, 1963, with a planting of a tree in the Avenue of the Righteous at Yad Vashem. Wladyslaw Bartoszewski was at the event. He was a founder of the Polish resistance who organized an underground organization, comprised mostly of Catholics, to save Jews. He worked to provide false documents to Jews living outside the Warsaw ghetto. In the fall of 1942, he helped found an organization (Council for Aid to Jews) that saved many Jews from the gas chambers.

Der Totentanz
or The Blue Rain
(oil on canvas, 48" x 36")

Naked and shorn, husband and wife dance in a final embrace in Zyklon B's blue crystal deadly rain.

Rain, rain—blue rain
Go away

Rain, rain—blue rain
Never come
Again.

Zyklon B was a commercial gas form of hydrocyanic acid, which became active on contact with air. It was manufactured by a firm called Degesch, which was largely owned by I.G. Farben, and brought to Auschwitz in the summer of 1941 as a vermin-killer and disinfectant.

Rudolf Höss, commandant of Auschwitz, spoke of the effect of the gas: "The door would now be quickly screwed up and the gas discharged by the waiting disinfectors through vents in the ceilings of the gas chambers, down a shaft that led to the floor. This insured the rapid distribution of the gas. It could be observed through the peephole in the door that those who were standing nearest to the induction vents were killed at once. It can be said that about one-third died straightaway. The remainder staggered about and began to scream and struggle for air. The screaming, however, soon changed to the death rattle and in a few minutes all lay still... The door was opened half an hour after the induction of the gas, and the ventilation switched on... The special detachment now set about removing the gold teeth and cutting the hair from the women. After this, the bodies were taken up by elevator and laid in front of the ovens, which had meanwhile been stoked up. Depending on the size of the bodies, up to three corpses could be put into one oven at the same time. The time required for cremation... took twenty minutes."

The Transmutations of Dr. Mengele
Children into Angels
(oil on canvas, 60" x 36")

Mengele used for his pseudoscientific experiments human guinea pigs, infants, young twins and dwarfs. Some of the experiments were made on their genital organs; they were given a variety of harmful injections, some directly into the heart. Most of the children died a cruel death.

Dr. Josef Mengele was known in Auschwitz as "The Angel of Death" because of his lethal experiments, primarily on twins. As member of the NS-Institute for Erbbiologie und Rassenhygiene (Hereditary Biology and Racial Hygiene), he joined the Waffen-SS voluntarily and worked as medical officer in France and the Soviet Union, where he received high distinctions before he was declared unsuitable for the front after an injury. In 1943, he went to Auschwitz—again voluntarily—in order to conduct medical and anthropological examinations, and was therefore supported by the Deutsche Forschungsgemeinschaft.

Priority of his "research" was a fanatically pursued "research on twins." Obviously, he wanted to verify the hereditary influences on people. Each twin-couple could be observed under the same life conditions, and sent to death in best health—an ideal assumption for post-mortal research. Other fields of his "research" were the examinations of Lilliputians as examples of the "Abnormal" and the "Nomal"—illness of cheeks that was caused by physical and psychical exhaustion. Shortly before the evacuation of Auschwitz, he returned to Günzburg, where he was not prevented from building up the firm of Carl Mengele and Sons again. It was in the mid-50s that the author Ernst Schnabel made Mengele an object of public discussion with his publication about Anne Frank. However, Mengele already had been gone to South America. He was never sent to Germany, and presumably died in a drowning accident in Brazil, in 1979.

Quo Vadis Germania?
What Hat Next?
(oil on canvas, 48" x 36")

Passion of Christ: "Simon Peter said to him [Jesus], 'Lord, where are you going? [Quo Vadis?]' Jesus answered him, 'Where I am going you cannot follow Me now, but you shall follow Me afterward.'" (from John 13:36)

People and their basic instincts have not changed since the beginning of time. They only have adjusted to the changing ecological, social and economic conditions of their particular surroundings. Present day humanity's behavior and actions are still motivated by the same Seven Deadly Sins as those of the stone-age people.

Applying the theory of probability, one must conclude that, given the same social, geopolitical and economic conditions existing at the time of the Weimar Republic, history will repeat itself. What hat next? *The Atomic Pickelhaube*?

Fritz Hirschberger